… THE RISE AND FALL OF EMPIRES

THE RISE AND FALL OF THE ROMAN EMPIRE

LISA IDZIKOWSKI

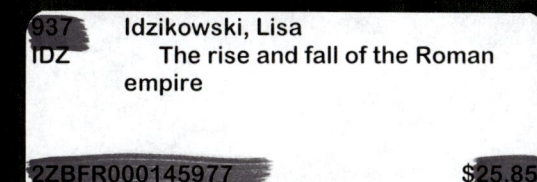

937 Idzikowski, Lisa
IDZ The rise and fall of the Roman empire

2ZBFR000145977 $25.85

ROSEN
PUBLISHING

Published in 2017 by The Rosen Publishing Group, Inc.
29 East 21st Street, New York, NY 10010

Copyright © 2017 by The Rosen Publishing Group, Inc.

First Edition

All rights reserved. No part of this book may be reproduced in any form without permission in writing from the publisher, except by a reviewer.

Library of Congress Cataloging-in-Publication Data
Names: Idzikowski, Lisa, author.
Title: The rise and fall of the Roman empire / Lisa Idzikowski.
Description: First edition. | New York, NY : Rosen Publishing Group, Inc., 2017. | Series: The rise and fall of empires | Includes bibliographical references and index. | Audience: Grade 7 to 12._
Identifiers: LCCN 2015048845| ISBN 9781499463323 (library bound) | ISBN
   9781499463309 (pbk.) | ISBN 9781499463316 (6-pack)
Subjects: LCSH: Rome—History—Empire, 30 B.C.-476 A.D.
Classification: LCC DG270 .I39 2016 | DDC 937/.06—dc23
LC record available at http://lccn.loc.gov/2015048845

Manufactured in China

Contents

Introduction 4

CHAPTER 1
Kings Along the Tiber River 6

CHAPTER 2
Rome Without Kings 13

CHAPTER 3
Desperate for Peace 26

CHAPTER 4
Times: They Are Changing 39

Timeline 53
Glossary 55
For More Information 56
For Further Reading 58
Bibliography 59
Index 61

INTRODUCTION

The Roman Empire, the ancient world's largest empire, was in some ways the world's first superpower. From the misty borders of the British Isles to the steamy banks of the Nile River in Egypt, at the height of the empire in 117 CE, its geographical area had engulfed a large portion of Europe, a parcel of Asia, and a piece of northern Africa. It reached far and wide, populated by fifty to sixty million people, covering up to 2 million square miles (5,179,976 square kilometers) of land, and requiring up to 53,000 miles (85,295 km) of roads to cover the territory.

From its agricultural beginnings, ancient Rome went through many centuries of change, innovation, and survival to become a cultural giant of the ancient world. Years of intense fighting and warring were interspersed with times of peace and prosperity. Through three fairly distinctive periods including an early beginning, middle republic, and later empire, Romans developed ideas, services, and systems that helped maintain and expand their world. Many continue to influence our modern lives although we may or may not recognize them. In today's languages, laws and government, water systems, architectural and construction styles, and literature and art reside the glimmerings of the Roman past, reaching down through the ages.

Many historians, both modern and ancient would agree that we continue to benefit from the experiences, experiments, and examples of the Roman civilization, which flourished for about five hundred years.

From earliest times, Rome fought and expanded its territories, and at its largest expanse it included parts of Europe, Asia, and northern Africa.

Chapter 1

Kings Along the Tiber River

Descending from the center of Europe, the long peninsula of Italy stakes its claim as it plunges southward into the Mediterranean Sea. The mighty Alps form a mountainous northern border separating it from the rest of Europe, while another sturdy mountain chain, the Apennines, marches the entire length of Italy's land mass. Since it is a rather narrow peninsula, the sea is never very far from any coastal shore.

EARLIEST CULTURE AND GEOGRAPHY OF ITALIC PEOPLE

Day after day, month after month, season after season, the sun shone upon the many distinct settlements of Latins, Etruscans, Umbrians, Sabines, Faliscans, Samnites, and others living in Italy. By about 900 BCE, many of these agricultural people constructed villages of simple huts and lived in small groups of individuals and families. As

Kings Along the Tiber River

farmers, they grew and harvested grain such as wheat and barley, and raised and consumed goats, pigs, sheep, and cattle. They also spoke their own languages and practiced their own forms of arts and crafts.

As these early tribes prospered, their numbers increased, and their villages grew. All throughout the Italian peninsula, groups of early Italic people were growing, gathering, and separating themselves into distinctive cultures. Eventually, they developed the ability to take iron ore from the earth and transform it into various objects. This Iron Age technology had a positive impact on their lives and added to the types of tools already being made from bone, stone, and wood.

This necropolis, or cemetery, was built and used by the Etruscan peoples, one of the many groups that lived on the Italian peninsula.

ROME AT LAST

One of the Latin groups had chosen as their settlement site an area overlooking one of Italy's large rivers, the Tiber. Besides being near a source of good, fresh water, these people sensed they should settle in an area that could be easily defended from others when necessary. Not a city yet,

The Rise and Fall of the Roman Empire

FROM THE MISTS OF TIME

Rome's ancient writers told the city's mythical beginning in two colorful tales of heroes, war, and escape. One version is from the *Aeneid*, an epic poem written by Rome's foremost poet, Virgil. According to Virgil, twin brothers Romulus and Remus were descendants of Aeneas, a prince of Troy who had escaped the Trojan War. After escaping, Aeneas fled to a distant land, settled there, and his descendants, Romulus and Remus, founded the city of Rome.

The other founding myth has Romulus and Remus as sons born to a mortal woman and the Roman god Mars.

Legendary founders of Rome Romulus and Remus are suckled by the she-wolf that found and saved them from certain death.

Kings Along the Tiber River

> Soon after birth the twins are put into a basket and thrown into the Tiber River. Instead of drowning, the basket reaches the shore, and the infants are found by a female wolf that saves the babies by bringing them to her lair and suckling them with her milk. One day a local shepherd discovers the boys and takes them home to raise them properly as his own sons. The story continues, and after Romulus and Remus are grown, they settle near the spot at the Tiber where they had once washed ashore. One day they have a terrible quarrel about who should rule the settlement. Romulus ends up killing his brother and names the city Rome, after himself.

the population grew and expanded in and around a group of hills situated above the river. Living at a higher elevation gave these villagers an advantage, and they continued to build and develop near two hills in particular: the Palatine and the Capitoline. Archaeologists have uncovered further evidence to suggest that by about 800 BCE this settlement on the Tiber was becoming more like a city—more organized, more populous, and more in contact with other distant communities and settlements—and they see this period in time as the beginning of Rome.

According to tradition, ancient Rome originated in 753 BCE (although it was more likely earlier), and this year marks the start of the monarchy of seven kings. Romulus, Rome's first king, founded the city, began some of its important political institutions, and ruled until 715 BCE.

The Rise and Fall of the Roman Empire

WEATHER-RESISTANT STONE SOUP

Gigantic, graceful structures filled Rome since early times. Engineers have uncovered their secret—*opus caementicium*, a Roman concrete. When hardened, its soupy stone formula made structures such as the magnificent Pantheon and Colosseum resistant to weathering. Archaeologists know that the Romans began concrete projects by the second century BCE and probably had been experimenting with it for years.

Roman concrete is a mixture of burnt limestone, water, chunks of brick or rock—and volcanic ash. Thanks to their secret ingredient, modern eyes can feast on what ancient people must have gazed at in wonder!

During Romulus's reign, a very prominent and important advisory group took shape, the Roman Senate. Numa Pompilius, Rome's second king, organized religious life and oversaw some of the early building in the city. The next two kings were Tullus Hostilius and Ancus Marcius. Hostilius actively fought with nearby towns and ruled until 642 BCE. Marcius, ruling until 617 BCE, oversaw the construction of a bridge over the Tiber. Directly following were Rome's last three kings, Lucius Tarquinius Priscus, Servius Tullius, and Lucius Tarquinius Superbus.

Kings Along the Tiber River

As the chosen gathering site of Rome, the Forum Romanum contained many structures dedicated to governmental, religious, and community functions.

ROME'S RELIGION AND CULTURE

Disagreements, skirmishes, and conquests were frequent events between the Romans and the many Italic peoples surrounding them during the reign of kings. But they also shared major concerns in daily life, such as religion and culture. Starting in the seventh century BCE, many buildings of religious and community significance were erected. Temples dedicated to Jupiter, Juno, Vulcan, Diana, and Vesta appeared. In addition to these major gods, many Romans revered and worshipped personal or household gods at shrines or small altars in their homes. The Romans also adopted religious beliefs and practices from surrounding neighbors. They

The Rise and Fall of the Roman Empire

This relief of Jupiter, Pluto, Persephone, Neptune, and Amphitrite (shown from left to right) depicts several of the gods and goddesses worshipped by Romans.

acquired a belief that images of various ducks and woodpeckers were sacred. (A woodpecker is said to have saved the infants Romulus and Remus along with a wolf.) Another common practice that the Romans borrowed from the Umbrians involved finding religious meaning in natural phenomena, such as formations of flying birds or claps of thunder during thunderstorms.

In the valley of Rome's hills, workers drained a swampy area and readied the ground for building. At this site, the Forum Romanum was situated along with several large stone buildings. Here the community had a central gathering place where people voted, participated in ceremonies, and assembled for public meetings. Workmen later built the Curia Hostilia, which the council of elders, the Senate, used for its meetings.

With Rome's population growing and expanding, its religious observances thriving, and its citizens flourishing, the sun would dawn on a bright new day.

CHAPTER 2

ROME WITHOUT KINGS

Toward the end of the sixth century BCE, with about thirty-five thousand people, Rome was well on its way to becoming a city of grand cultural mix and wealth. Romans continued conquering and assimilating neighboring cities, making changes to some local customs and ideas before incorporating the people and culture into their own.

GRAND CITY BEFORE THE REPUBLIC

Citizens of a city often had different roles or jobs within that city to keep it running smoothly. Rome was no different. A king still ruled with absolute power, but he had others to help. The *populus Romanus*—the free-born (not slave) adult men of Rome—helped conduct the affairs of the city. Another group firmly rooted in Roman society was a social class called the patricians. This group of powerful, elite, wealthy families had been present since the beginning of Rome.

The Rise and Fall of the Roman Empire

Patricians believed that they as individuals were special simply by being born into one of these elite, wealthy families. From earliest times, their aims of power, wealth, and control guided their actions. To grab this lead in society and keep it, they made sure that their men filled the army, became priests, and held most other important community jobs. And to be a member of the Senate, the most powerful group of men in Rome besides the king, a man had to be patrician-born. The Senate imagined itself as a powerful advisory board to the king. Some kings sought advice and aimed to please the Senate; others openly shunned and disregarded its decisions.

Politicians often addressed the Roman Senate. Here, Cato the Censor tries to persuade senators to agree on all-out war against the city of Carthage.

Rome Without Kings

NO KINGS, NOW WHAT?

At the closing of the sixth century BCE, around 509 BCE, the rule of the last of the Roman kings, Lucius Tarquinius Superbus, or Tarquin the Proud, ended. Historians write that members of the patrician class overthrew Tarquin because he was a tyrant and that he and members of his family had committed various crimes. The rule of kings was no more; the new age of the Roman Republic had begun.

A general feeling that many Romans held dear was that they as a people were predestined to rule over others. Romans believed that this power was bestowed upon them by their gods. In order to fulfill this assumption of predestination, they aimed to perfect certain personal qualities. In turn, they expected their elected officials to demonstrate these same values of courage, strength, and excellence.

In the early years of the Roman Republic, Rome was governed by elected officials called magistrates. Eventually, to replace the king, the two highest ranking magistrates, called consuls, were elected to serve one-year terms. They took charge of the government and the army. Each consul had the power to overrule the other, in effect preventing any more monarchs. But who exactly elected these consuls? Groups comprised of the *populus Romanus*, called assemblies, voted and elected the consuls. And even though all free-born men could participate in these elections, the votes of men from the wealthy and elite families counted more toward the final selection. Consequently, the patrician class maintained an upper hand in governing Rome.

This continual uneven distribution of power created much ill-will and anger among the people. In the general population of Rome most people belonged to one of the three distinct strata of citizens: patricians, plebeians, or "plebs," and slaves. The elite patrician class had organized themselves into two groups, the *senatores*, or members of the Senate, and the *equites*—still powerful but not automatically in the Senate. The plebeians, or common people, made up the largest portion of Roman society, and the slaves, at the lowest level of society, were mostly outsiders who had been captured in conquests. Slavery was commonplace. Patrician families might have hundreds of slaves, while even the poorest plebeian families owned one or two. Slaves came from many walks of life and worked as personal servants, laborers, craftspeople, clerks, and even teachers and doctors. Industrious slaves could work hard, save their money, and eventually buy their freedom into the society.

The plebeians' lesser power put them in a position of almost constant struggle against the patricians. One of their demands involved having Roman civil laws put into writing. Up until this time, Rome's laws were not written down; they were known and transmitted orally. The plebeians' persistence won out. Around the middle of the fifth century BCE, a special group tackled this task. Consequently, a set of written laws, the Laws of the Twelve Tables, was produced. The Twelve Tables detailed laws pertaining to marriage, divorce, ownership of land, and other rights needed for a mainly agricultural society.

Rome Without Kings

Romans had another guide to shape their knowledge of acceptable personal behavior. Through the paterfamilias, or male head of the household—typically the father or grandfather—people learned to obey the values and rules of Roman society. If someone exhibited completely unacceptable behavior, the paterfamilias could even control whether or not that family member would live or die.

Household slaves cooked daily meals as part of their duties and often prepared elaborate feasts.

NEVER-ENDING WAR

Strong feelings emerged at the beginning of Rome's Republic among the people of many of its surrounding cultures and communities. They sensed that without a king, wealthy, powerful Rome might be vulnerable. This set the stage for continuous conflict. In general, Romans reacted in one of two different ways: many times they engaged rivals in vicious battles, but at other times, they also tried to convince challengers to join the republic. Some groups, especially smaller communities, surrendered, but many opted for war.

The Rise and Fall of the Roman Empire

Because there was so much conflict, Rome needed a large, well-organized army. In the early years of the republic, magistrates called military tribunes performed several important duties in service. They chose men from the adult population to serve as soldiers. The tribunes also carefully honored and made sacrifices to the gods. After all, Romans believed they would achieve victory with the gods' favor. In the event of war, men quit their farms or regular occupations, and, with weapons and armor that they had purchased themselves, followed their commanders into battle. With discipline and determination they conquered many, but not all of their opponents.

Besides winning or losing for the republic, commanders and soldiers often

In the Roman army, centurions, or officers like the one here, took charge of the day-to-day functioning of legions, the large military groups of armed soldiers.

Rome Without Kings

suffered consequences, both good and bad. Many soldiers were farmers, and depending on the timing of battles, they might lose their harvest if they were away at war. They could also gain extra land or other types of wealth as part of war bounty. Patricians, as commanders or leaders, more often found they gained from the experience either added wealth or prestige, especially when victorious in battle.

Fighting continued over many, many years, and at times seemed endless. Rome expanded its geographic and cultural area and either conquered or made allies of neighboring and outlying communities. The citizens of some conquered towns were granted Roman citizenship with complete rights, including the vote. Rome gave others limited citizenship, while still others received ally status. In some instances, especially if the fight had been brutal or long and continuous, Roman commanders might destroy the towns and take prisoners. Romans could be brutal, but in certain instances, they preferred to use persuasion and have willing allies. At times, the Romans practiced the belief of *fides*, or good faith, which meant they needed to use personal constraint and not impose excessively harsh conditions upon those they conquered.

By about 300 BCE many of the surrounding tribes and communities had either lost their fight or had submitted to Roman rule. One group held out. It seemed that Rome could do nothing to persuade the Samnites to end the continuous combat in which they were engaged. The Samnites were a fierce fighting faction who would rather die than

The Rise and Fall of the Roman Empire

surrender. Rome's armies had fought the Samnites several times before these warriors managed to convince the Gauls, Etruscans, and Umbrians to join together in a last stand for independence. It was an all-out, everybody against Rome attack—and Rome emerged victorious.

WHY STOP NOW?

Before long, Rome dominated the Italian peninsula. Did Rome's appetite for expansion cease? Hardly. Starting in the mid-third century BCE, it became involved in three long wars—called the Punic Wars—against another very powerful city of the time. Carthage, in present-day Tunisia, controlled a large area including the islands of Sicily and Sardinia and the lands of northern Africa and parts of Spain. At the conclusion of the Punic Wars, the city of Carthage would no longer be what it was.

The First Punic War began in 264 BCE when a unit of Carthaginian soldiers clashed with citizens in Sicily. Rome was called on to help Sicily, and very soon, a major conflict raged. Battles were fought on land and sea with Rome being at a severe disadvantage in the beginning. Carthage had a strong navy. Rome had none. Some villages and towns sided with the Romans, and some with the Carthaginians. Rome quickly built a navy and devised naval tactics for battle. In about twenty years, the first Punic War ended with Rome as victor.

Rome Without Kings

In 218 BCE, the Second Punic War erupted after a disagreement over a city in present-day Spain. An attack by Carthage's famous war general, Hannibal, meant that Rome was called on to help once again. Armies from Rome marched on foot and sailed by sea. Vicious fighting and wins and losses for both armies prolonged the conflict. Suddenly, the Roman forces were completely surprised. Hannibal crossed the Alps and staged his successes with unusual help—a troop of elephants!

Hannibal, his soldiers, and his elephants trekked and

In 218 BCE, Carthaginian general Hannibal fought against Rome in the Second Punic War. His arsenal included a large number of men and weapons and about three dozen elephants.

tracked down through the Italian peninsula. Back and forth, back and forth both sides fought. Rome resorted to a general tactic of wearing down Hannibal's forces. Finally, Rome sent a brilliant commander to northern Africa to take the

ROME'S INFORMATION AND MILITARY HIGHWAY

Just how did the Roman armies manage to get around their expanding territory to engage in all these battles? They marched tirelessly, covering up to 20 miles (32 km) a day over roads built by some of the earliest expert road builders in history! But, to set the record straight, the legions were likely often passed by speeding imperial couriers who raced around Rome's territories on horseback, traveling up to 60 miles (96.5 km) a day carrying vital information and collecting taxes.

Roman roads were plotted and constructed by top engineers over fields, around rivers, straight through mountains, and up hills. Users traveled over the layered constructs and easily followed signage to guide them along the way. Special army troops, the *stationarii*, guarded against robbers and other problems, and horse changing stations made it possible to exchange tired mounts for a fresh set of legs.

In 312 BCE, the Via Appia, or Appian Way was created to enable the army to move from Rome to Capua during the second war against the Samnites. Incredibly, some of these roads, with their bridges and tunnels, are still in use today!

fight directly to Carthage, Hannibal's own city. Of course Hannibal rushed home to defend his city, but his efforts were in vain. Hannibal and his armies suffered defeat at the hands of the Romans.

Not surprisingly, arguments, skirmishes, and battles continued after the end of the Second Punic War. As Rome maintained its superiority over Carthage and new provinces in Spain, it began expanding into other Mediterranean areas. In 149 BCE Rome was called upon yet again, to a dispute. According to historical reports, exaggerated claims against Carthage by members of Rome's Senate and from a northern African king might have prompted Rome to intervene. As Rome had often done, it rushed to battle with Carthage, for the Third Punic War. Roman forces killed and enslaved many Carthaginians, and Carthage itself finally fell.

LIFE BEYOND WAR

Did nothing but war interest, concern, or delight the Romans? Just like people today, the citizens of Rome and the Italian peninsula loved, laughed, worshipped, and wondered. They prayed to their gods, read and enjoyed poetry and plays, and marveled at colossal architecture.

Religion played a central part in everyday life—for everyone. All throughout the city and countryside, public and private temples, altars, and sacred groves filled various locations. Grand public temples had been built early on to encourage and support sacrifice and worship to

THE RISE AND FALL OF THE ROMAN EMPIRE

Worship of Vesta, Roman goddess of the hearth, took place in the Temple of Vesta. Priestesses tended a sacred burning flame, believed to ensure Rome's survival.

Jupiter, Juno and Minerva—Rome's three most vital gods.

Romans worshipped and adored another important deity, Vesta, goddess of the hearth. In these agricultural times, a well-tended hearth proved a necessity. Not only for cooking, warmth, and light, a home's fire provided a comfortable gathering spot. Through prayers and sacrifices to Vesta, a family would be guaranteed a perpetual fire and success in family life. In public the grand Temple of Vesta supported her adoration. Six young women, the Vestal Virgins, tended a sacred fire that, when

Rome Without Kings

kept burning, promised continued prosperity and good fortune for Rome.

Families also worshipped gods and spirits that represented parts of the home, possessions, and ancestors. An interesting aspect of Romans' worship involved the practice of making promises to the gods. A person would perform the promised devotion only after the gods themselves first granted the wishes of the individual.

Several fine authors wrote at this time. Ancient historians recorded the events of Rome and also preserved descriptions of festivals, usually—but not always—associated with religious observances. Charioteers and races, dancers, musicians, and dramatic performances provided entertainment. Poets and playwrights pleased their followers with epic poems and prose as well as tragic and comedic plays.

Temples dedicated to religious worship stood out for their splendid architecture. However other structures, such as those for food storage and water provisions, were also significant. The famed Roman aqueducts, built both underground and above ground, transported water across Rome. Additional aqueducts were built in many of Rome's territories. Remnants of some of these impressive structures can still be seen today.

All in all, the Roman Republic was expanding and would continue to do so for some time.

Chapter 3

DESPERATE FOR PEACE

By late in Rome's republican period, all of Italy, much of Spain, southern France, northern Africa, and nearby islands were under Roman rule. Conquest continued and by the first century BCE, Greece and Asia Minor had joined the list of provinces. Rome, without a doubt, had become the most powerful domain on earth.

NOT ALL ROSY IN THE LATER REPUBLIC

Cracks developed in this pedestal of power: greed and lust for power fueled the ambitions of consuls and military commanders; soldiers pledged allegiance to their commanders instead of the state; the wealthy concerned themselves with acquiring luxury at others' expense; and the common people's suffering became overwhelming.

Disagreements, fighting, and even murders among the Senate and representatives of the plebeian assemblies

DESPERATE FOR PEACE

symbolized dire contrasts in the republic. The consuls and the Senate fought to retain and increase their control. In the meantime, the elected magistrates of Rome's common people, Rome's allies, and Rome's provinces insisted they have a greater share in governing.

A volatile mix of influences overcame Rome, and something had to be done. Three generals, Julius Caesar, Gaius Pompey, and Marcus Crassus, banded together. Forming the First Triumvirate, they determined to act together and halt the chaos. At first it worked, but then Crassus died in battle. Caesar and Pompey found themselves facing off and vying for control.

Civil war followed, with many senators backing Pompey. Caesar persevered, and his legions eventually defeated Pompey's forces. He then became Rome's dictator, a position that differed from that of a king (as Romans no longer wanted a monarchy in power) and gave him sole authority over Rome and its provinces. As dictator, Caesar wanted to make Rome great again. In 49 BCE, with this goal in mind, he attempted to employ Roman citizens seeking jobs and to give land in the outlying colonies to those who had none. Caesar tried to bring knowledgeable lawyers, doctors, and intellectuals to Rome from areas around the Mediterranean. In his few short years in charge, he became the first living Roman to have his image on coins. He also had the calendar rearranged to reflect a true solar year. Toward the end of Caesar's short rule, senators became extremely angry at their diminished power. Eventually, they plotted and killed Caesar on March 15, 44 BCE.

THE RISE AND FALL OF THE ROMAN EMPIRE

Enraged over Caesar's power and popularity, a group of Roman senators plotted his assassination. On March 15, 44 BCE, two assassins stabbed Caesar to death.

ROME'S EMPIRE: PEACE WITHIN REACH

Before his death, Caesar officially adopted his great-nephew, Gaius Octavius, or Octavian. As Caesar's heir, Octavian could only guess about his future. He probably never imagined that at age eighteen he would become ruler of Rome and usher in a long period of peace and prosperity.

DESPERATE FOR PEACE

After Caesar's demise, Octavian initially joined forces with two magistrates, Mark Antony and Marcus Lepidus. As Rome's Second Triumvirate, the Senate granted them control over Rome for five years, ordered them to find Caesar's assassins, and made each responsible for different portions of Rome's far-reaching provinces. As in previous years, peaceful cooperation did not last.

Conflicts arose and in time, Octavian ruled in the west and Antony ruled in the east. Neither of the co-rulers could predict the vicious battles to come, in which citizens, soldiers, and senators alike chose sides. Antony even courted Egypt's queen, Cleopatra, in an all-out attempt to gain military supremacy and destroy Octavian and his legions. Octavian and his armies prevailed, and with the deaths of Antony and Cleopatra, he became sole ruler of the Roman world, marking Rome's transition from a republic to an empire.

On January 16, 27 BCE, Octavian became Augustus, the first emperor of Rome. Smart and very capable, Augustus did not emphasize his power even though he had the complete support of the army. He preferred to use the title *princeps civitatis*, or "first citizen," rather than emperor. Even though the Senate wished to heap many powers onto Augustus, he purposefully vowed to restore power to the Senate. The princeps carefully avoided appearing as a dictator in charge of Rome.

Augustus clearly wanted to steer Rome back to peace and prosperity. He focused on winning approval from the Senate, the army, and the mass of ordinary citizens.

The Rise and Fall of the Roman Empire

Augustus showed interest in senatorial matters, respected senators' wishes, and made them feel they were in charge of the empire. He abolished the draft and created a professional army that swore allegiance to the state. Augustus also engaged in building, expanding, and improving many projects benefitting most of Rome's population, including temples, aqueducts, and roads. The princeps cared for the poor by attempting to increase the amount of free grain given to the people. And he encouraged the elite families in particular to return to the respected practices from Rome's earlier times in matters of marriage and child rearing.

A golden age of literature also blossomed under Augustus's reign. He and other wealthy men sponsored and supported several well-known writers. Three poets, Virgil, Ovid, and Horace enjoyed popularity at this time. Virgil composed epics, Ovid created poems

As Caesar's adopted heir, Gaius Octavius took the name Augustus when he assumed control of Rome and ruled for many years as its first emperor.

DESPERATE FOR PEACE

about love, and Horace crafted his *Odes*. Another author, Pliny, observed and recorded natural phenomenon in his book, *Natural History*.

Even though Augustus's reign was not devoid of conflict, because of his efforts and wise decisions in governing, the one million or so citizens of Rome at last found the peace that they so desperately needed. This age of peace and prosperity, called the Pax Romana, would go on to last for approximately two centuries.

Roman poet Virgil (*seated*) is joined by two muses, or goddesses of literary and artistic inspiration, as he writes his epic poem, the *Aeneid*.

THE GOOD, THE BAD, AND THE UGLY AFTER AUGUSTUS

After Augustus died in 14 CE, four emperors, all extended family members of his, followed. Each of the Julio-Claudian rulers demonstrated good, bad, and ugly tendencies while steering the ship of the Roman state.

Following Augustus's death, his adopted stepson Tiberius assumed power. Tiberius had been chosen by Augustus himself, but he never enjoyed the support of average Romans. He seemed secretive and rarely appeared at public functions. He acted in contradictory ways—generously giving money at times for people in need, but then having others deported from the city.

When Tiberius died in 37 CE, the great-grandson of Augustus promptly accepted the imperial power granted him by the Senate. At first, Gaius, nicknamed, Caligula, was well-liked. He encouraged the Senate to exercise power, attended chariot races, and began constructing new projects such as roads and aqueducts.

Suddenly, things changed dramatically. Historians believe Caligula may have suffered a serious fever that altered his mind. His moods and decisions turned sour and his actions became unpredictable. Caligula argued all the time, ordered multiple murders, and appointed his horse as consul. In 41 CE, Caligula's own guards struck him down.

Caligula's uncle Claudius stepped up to fill Rome's imperial spot. The Praetorian Guard—essentially the

DESPERATE FOR PEACE

emperor's bodyguards—that had assassinated Caligula hailed Claudius as the new princeps. Some senators and elite could not accept this development. Claudius suffered from physical disabilities and deformities thought to be caused by illnesses during youth. Many people assumed he also suffered from limited mental capabilities, but Claudius surprised them.

Like Augustus, Claudius encouraged military campaigns. He even directed the successful invasion into Britain. Claudius built many roads, aqueducts, and temples, and when grain seemed to be in very short supply, he urged merchants to find ways to obtain more. Unfortunately, the emperor did not always predict what his family members plotted. Some writers of the time maintain that his third wife poisoned him after Claudius adopted her son, Nero, as his heir.

Nero rose to power in 54 CE, after Claudius's poisoning. As a young man of sixteen, Nero needed direction. His tutor, a member of the Praetorian Guard, and his mother advised him in the beginning. Interestingly, the arts interested the emperor instead of government and the military. The first five years of his reign appeared fine, but after that he began a murderous spree, either ordering killings or suicides. He even boasted that he might have the entire Senate done away with. All this combined with the Jewish Revolt in Judaea (part of modern Israel) and several uprisings scattered throughout regions that are in present-day Germany, Britain, and France caused the Senate to declare Nero a public enemy. Soon afterwards Nero committed suicide.

The Rise and Fall of the Roman Empire

Many citizens enjoyed a better quality of life in the first century CE of Imperial Rome despite such events as the great fire of 64, which happened during Nero's rule, and the eruption of Mount Vesuvius, which followed in 79 CE. Most Roman lands were peaceful, with the majority of the army active only on the borders far away. Outside Rome, farming and agriculture kept a large part of the population busy and working. The trading economy increased as the wealthy elite sought and purchased luxury items, while citizens purchased useful products for their everyday lives. Grand construction projects, such as the great amphitheater and the Colosseum—for which Rome remains well-known—advanced during this time. Roads and harbors also developed.

Of some concern was the large portion of the population of Rome both unemployed and extremely poor or well enough off that they had little to occupy themselves. Some leaders worried that people with too much free time might become

The emperor Vespasian started building of the great amphitheater in Rome, known today as the Colosseum, where wild animal and gladiatorial fights took place.

DESPERATE FOR PEACE

ROME'S GODS, NOT FOR EVERYONE

What happens when different groups worship different gods? In the Roman Empire there was generally tolerance for different religious practices, including the worship of different gods. Very early in the first century CE, the Romans ruled over the province of Judaea, in what is now part of Jerusalem. Romans and a large Jewish population lived in the community. Before mid-century, many religious men roamed the countryside preaching their own set of beliefs. This led to various struggles. Relations between Jewish and non-Jewish neighbors and rulers were usually good, but these deteriorated, disagreements increased, and riots soon followed.

One of the preachers, a man named Jesus Christ, was seen as a big problem. Eventually he was branded a criminal and sentenced to die by Judaea's governor. After his death, Jesus's followers continued preaching his message to many, many people. Some of his followers broke away from the Jewish faith and formed a new religion, Christianity.

Difficulties intensified, and in 66 CE riots broke out in Judaea. Rebellions grew worse, and four years later, the Roman army smashed the Jewish fighters, killing many of them. Unfortunately, this did not end the troubles between Rome and the Jews. Two additional revolts beginning in 115 and 132 CE attempted to eradicate followers of the Jewish faith.

dissatisfied in some way and revolt. Consequently, a plan to furnish free food and entertainment expanded. Bread, grain, and other food, plus a wide variety of leisure time activities became commonly available. *Ludi*, or celebrations, both religious and secular, crowded the calendar. Feasts, chariot races, parades, gladiatorial contests, and wild animal shows and fights took place during times of celebration. And public baths, much like modern-day health clubs, sprang up around the city.

Several individuals ruled in the period between Nero's death and the late first century. And a very important law, which enabled the emperor to grant patrician status to men not from traditional elite families, came into effect. Men from Spain, northern Italy, Greece, and North Africa then became senators. Change was slowly coming to Rome, but the best was to come as Roman culture marched toward the end of the first century.

THE GOOD, THE BETTER, THE BEST FIVE EMPERORS

At the very end of the first century, Rome perched on the edge of an exceptional period—the time of five great emperors. With their rule, various military campaigns occurred, the economy prospered, the Pax Romana continued, and the empire grew to its greatest size.

Marcus Cocceius Nerva, the first of the five, never expected to become emperor. Nerva right away started to

DESPERATE FOR PEACE

show his worth as ruler. He worked well with and respected the Senate and even took an oath never to have any senators killed. He also contributed money so that landless citizens in Rome and Italy could acquire their own plots, and poor families could have help for their children.

Shortly before he died, Nerva adopted the next emperor to be. Marcus Ulpius Trajanus was special. He was the first ruler from the provinces—born and raised in Spain. Down through history, Trajan became known as *Optimus Princeps,* or "best ruler." His actions as emperor made him well liked by all. The army and Senate supported Trajan, and common people accepted his monetary gifts. To pay for his generosity and building spree of aqueducts, roads, canals, and ports, he advanced conquest for economic gain. Trajan's armies marched into and conquered Dacia, in

This detailed section of the much larger sculpted Trajan's Column illustrates the successful military campaigns of Trajan's army during the Dacian Wars.

modern day Romania. He then achieved his aim: to control, develop, and reap the riches of Dacia's gold, silver, and iron mines. In turn, Dacia became a flourishing province of the empire. During a military excursion to parts of the Middle East, Trajan died.

Shortly before his death, Trajan adopted his relative Publius Aelius Hadrianus, so Hadrian could assume the right to rule. Hadrian showed an interest in military matters and intellectual pursuits. He opted for security of the borders rather than further expansion. He traveled throughout the empire all during his reign, meeting with both local elites and commoners. Hadrian saw to the construction of a network of walls and forts to protect Rome's far borders in Britain and the completion of the Pantheon, one of Rome's most enduring structures.

The last rulers of this illustrious group essentially continued the work of the previous three. Hadrian's successor, Antoninus Pius, shared the ideas of his predecessors toward social welfare for the poor and underprivileged, and basically kept up the well-run empire. Following Pius's death, two men ruled jointly for a brief time until, Marcus Aelius Aurelius assumed sole control. During Marcus Aurelius's reign, soldiers fighting in the Persian Gulf area contracted a virulent contagion. As they made their way back home, the illness spread throughout the empire and raged for about twenty-five years, killing countless millions.

Unfortunately, this mysterious infection only hinted at the troubles to come.

Chapter 4

Times: They Are Changing

Perhaps the spread of deathly contagions robbed Romans of their feelings of well-being. Undoubtedly, years of battle between a multitude of army commanders for the chance to rule the empire contributed. Masses of countryside people joined the already overcrowded, suffering lot of the poor in cities. Whatever the cause, a generalized state of anxiety became evident starting with the end of the Pax Romana around 180 CE.

CENTURY OF CRISIS

Multiple problems and changes surfaced at this time in the Roman world. Some took place comparatively quickly, while others were gradual and continous over generations. The speedy turnover of generally incompetent rulers made it almost impossible for the army to act against a rash of border invasions. Many of these rulers and generals fought one another instead of their enemies. Barbarians, or non-Roman outsiders, came from different

The Rise and Fall of the Roman Empire

tribes but were believed to be uneducated, uncultured, and warlike by many Roman citizens. They repeatedly crossed over into Roman territory fighting every inch of the way. Much of this territorial skirmishing took place north and east of the great boundaries of the Rhine River and Danube River, which had been two of the main boundaries in the western part of the empire. At the same time, in the Persian Empire, which comprised modern-day Iraq and Iran, the Sasanians and their king began raiding nearby Roman towns of the eastern section, killing at will and taking slaves.

All the while life for average citizens of the realm continued to deteriorate. Food shortages and famine spread wide. The number of farmers and agricultural workers diminished, and consequently much of the outlying farmland sat vacant. Any available food supplies needed to go to the army and its soldiers. And because inflation had set in, money was not worth as much, and prices had climbed terribly; average people could not afford to buy the little amount of available food. With an undernourished population, disease typically set in. Yet again, a terrible illness struck the empire, and records indicate that around 262 CE, approximately five thousand people died daily in Rome from this contagion.

One construction project exemplified the feelings of many Romans of the time. Earlier, walls had been constructed all along the northern frontiers to keep the border intact. People then had confidence in their empire. They never dreamed of suffering the status of a conquered nation. When Hadrian's Wall was completed in 128 CE to try

Times: They Are Changing

Shapur I, king of the Sasanid Empire commemorates his victory in battle over Rome's emperor Valerian. On his knees, Valerian is forced to pay homage.

and keep Rome itself from being sacked, however, citizens began to fear the possibility of being overrun. It had turned out to be a century in crisis.

A TEMPORARY RALLY OF THE LATER EMPIRE

In 284 CE the Roman world rallied around a new ruler. The emperor Diocletian promptly initiated a series of changes

The Rise and Fall of the Roman Empire

at the start of Rome's Later Empire, which began around the late third and early fourth century. Almost at once, he encountered a great military challenge as most borders of the realm fell under intense attack. Diocletian realized that ruling an empire of Rome's size and directing its defenses was an impossible task for one man.

He appointed three other men to corule with him as a tetrarchy. Diocletian as augustus, or chief ruler, managed operations in the eastern section of the empire from Turkey with his caesar, or coruler. Maximian ruled as augustus in the west from northern Italy with his caesar. All four tetrarchs tackled threats of invasion throughout

Emperors Diocletian and Maximian (*seated on left*) look on as Saint Sebastian implores two brothers not to renounce their Christian beliefs.

Times: They Are Changing

the empire, especially in Egypt, Mesopotamia, Persia, and Britain.

Diocletian tried to improve the economy by enacting economic changes. He attempted to manage inflation by ordering price caps on goods and services that people bought and sold. He also forced individuals to remain in their jobs for life and tried to control the amount of pay they earned for their work. Roman money was not worth very much anymore because the coins were being made with cheap metals. To counter this decline in value, Diocletian ordered mints to forge coins containing larger percentages of pure silver and gold.

The emperor made adjustments to religious beliefs as well. He re-emphasized traditional religious practice, which mandated worship of Rome's pagan gods, particularly Jupiter and Hercules. With Diocletian's imposed sanctions, Christians came under intense scrutiny and punishment. Many Romans had always mistrusted Christians for a variety of reasons: they worshiped only one God and consequently refused to honor the emperor, preferred not to fight in the army, and believed in a promised afterlife. Consequently, Diocletian ordered the "Great Persecution" to begin throughout the empire. Churches, church leaders, and faithful followers were persecuted in various ways. Oppression of Christians became severe in the eastern part of the realm, with church leaders and followers eventually tortured and killed, sacred texts and churches destroyed, and others imprisoned. Curiously, the persecutions did not take hold in the western realm.

The Rise and Fall of the Roman Empire

Christians are about to be attacked and killed by wild animals as punishment for their beliefs, while Romans witness the spectacle in the Colosseum.

Eventually, illness forced Diocletian to give up power. In fact, he would be the first Roman emperor ever to leave office alive and looking forward to retirement. Before he left office, Diocletian tried to ensure the continuation of his idea of tetrarchy by proposing the next four tetrarchs. Unfortunately, his choices did not sit well with those involved. A power struggle erupted between Diocletian's appointees and their sons. As had happened so many times in Rome's history, fighting continued for years. The contenders engaged in battles not only against external enemies, but with each other.

By 312 CE, a defining battle took place between two of the tetrarchs' sons. Constantine and Maxentius, and their two armies fought just outside Rome's city walls. Constantine defeated his rival, killing Maxentius and many of his men. A curious story circulated after this conflict.

Times: They Are Changing

Historians differ on the exact truth, but Constantine supposedly experienced some sort of vision—possibly a cross in the sky—or dream prior to battle. He interpreted it as a message from heaven, and as a result ordered his soldiers to decorate their armor with a special Christian symbol. As Constantine's omen had promised, he and his soldiers emerged victorious from fighting.

Although Constantine credited the Christian god with help in battle, he remained a pagan. But the following year he demonstrated his gratitude with a proclamation. Constantine, ruler of the western realm, together with Licinius, a general in control of most of the eastern section, jointly issued the Edict of Milan, which promoted religious tolerance of all beliefs and religions, especially Christianity.

Not surprisingly, Constantine and Licinius did not remain content as ruling partners for long. Disagreements turned into disgust, which deteriorated into war. And yet again, Constantine and his army overwhelmingly defeated their opponents.

COULD THE EMPIRE PREVAIL?

After his latest victory, Constantine continued as sole emperor over east and west for thirteen years. Throughout this time he enacted laws and initiated procedures aiming to put cities back in better shape. Constantine's legislation favored Christians. In an attempt to make Rome a Christian city, he constructed a number of churches, hoping that the Christian religion would

The Rise and Fall of the Roman Empire

be seen as a legitimate practice instead of a cult to be scorned and feared.

But Constantine realized Rome's many shortcomings. Many people still strongly held pagan beliefs, and there was a dwindling population, an overtaxed economy, and an increasing disease rate. He knew that his capital should be elsewhere—in particular, he felt it should be closer to the geographical areas of border disputes. Wisely, Constantine relocated his power base east to Byzantium, the New Rome, in present-day Turkey. By 330 CE, he had enlarged the city, renamed it

As a longtime supporter of Christianity, Emperor Constantine finally joined the Christian faith by being baptized shortly before his death.

Times: They Are Changing

Constantinople—the city of Constantine—and dedicated it to the Christians' Virgin Mary.

The emperor did not have long to live, and close to death he took the final step of joining the Christian faith—Constantine was baptized. With his baptism in 337 CE, Christianity became accepted as a religion and gained many followers. Some practitioners of Christianity began feeling superior to pagan believers, and as a result, some pagan temples, statues, and shrines suffered destruction at the hands of Christians.

After the death of Constantine and with the end of the fourth century in the not-too-distant future, a sense of chaos caused by various difficulties, swept the empire. Several emperors, some Christian and some pagan, including a few relatives of Constantine, came and went. Some ruled by themselves, while others elected a joint ruler. In most instances, one ruled from a western city, while the other chose an eastern city. Importantly, the only governing body in Rome was the Senate.

Poverty and food shortages for common people had always occurred but now were almost intolerable, while wealthy families still enjoyed their comforts. More than ever, the west depended on the east.

THE UNIMAGINABLE

The year of Emperor Theodosius's death in 395 CE marked the complete division of the Roman Empire. There was a total split between east and west, total chaos in the western army, and total disintegration of the borders under barbarian attack. The western half was managed in many ways by individuals who were still part of the elite and wealthy families. Consequently, they often worked to their own advantage rather than for the common good. In contrast, members of the eastern civil service, comprised of common people, saw their jobs as a duty, which required them to work for the good of all. Economically and socially, the west continued its decline while the east forged ahead.

One of the worst problems for the west was that the army faced some calamitous issues, and because of these, the west was unable to defend against invasion. Military commanders still jockeyed for power and control, which was nothing new. But now they faced pressure to defend against the hordes of barbarians trying to fight their way into lands of the empire, which proved essentially impossible. The Huns, fierce, savage, warriors from central Asia, had whipped their horses into and across eastern Europe. Most other tribes in these affected areas feared the horrific horsemen and had hurried across the empire's borders to escape.

Average Roman citizens still disliked and distrusted the Germanic people. But Roman military commanders saw these new settlers as the remedy for a long-standing problem. For years, the number of army recruits had dropped dismally. What could be done to enlist enough soldiers? The Germanic clansmen were the answer. Some tribes were accepted as *foederati*,

Times: They Are Changing

or allies. They could then fight alongside established Roman armies against other tribal invaders.

Confusion soon overwhelmed the forces. At times, the foederati did fight against other Germans. However, at other times, they changed their minds and joined sides with the invading tribes and fought against the Romans. In essence, this left Rome, Italy, and the western provinces as open targets. Several Germanic generals took advantage of the situation.

Visigothic tribesmen led by Prince Alaric swarm into Rome and overrun its defenses. For the first time in over eight centuries, Rome was overthrown.

The Rise and Fall of the Roman Empire

SPOTLIGHT ON THE VISIGOTHS

Romans used the term "barbarian" when referring to people living outside the borders of the empire. Many Germanic people lived beyond the near and far borders, and the Visigoths were a group of tribes that made up a large segment of this population.

Not much is known about the Visigoths. Some tribes lived north of Rome's frontier border, the Danube River, northwest of the Black Sea, into modern-day Romania. Years of raids, frightful battles, negotiations, mistrust, and some peace, came and went between the Romans and the Visigoths.

Some tribes became allies, and their men fought with Rome against various invaders. Other times, the tribes fought bitterly against the empire and even attacked and looted the city of Rome.

By the end of the Western Roman Empire, the Visigoths had settled near modern day France and Spain. Their kingdom endured until about 700 CE.

ROME IS SACKED!

Rome was sacked not once, but twice. In 410 CE, Visigothic prince Alaric and his soldiers swarmed into Rome. For the first time in more than eight hundred years, Rome was overthrown. Conditions deteriorated further, and one by one, Roman provinces fell to Germanic invaders. First Britain, then Spain and North Africa—all were lost. Then

Times: They Are Changing

in 455 CE, the German king, Gaiseric the Vandal, led his warriors north from Africa, invaded Rome, and looted the city for about three weeks.

Roughly twenty years later, the city of Ravenna, capital of the Western Roman Empire, was overtaken by yet another German, General Flavius Odoacer. He and his warriors swept into the city, deposed the last Roman emperor, Romulus Augustulus, and Odoacer proclaimed himself *rex*, or king of all Italy. As king, Odoacer allowed the pope to remain in Rome. The pope, as head of the Catholic Church, served to be a powerful guide and stabilizing force for the fallen empire.

But, was this the end of the empire?

EMPIRE LIVES ON

Some historians would say that instead of disappearing, Rome evolved. They would argue that we witness the legacies of Rome in our lives every day.

Because the Roman Catholic Church continued using Latin, the language flourished, and through the years, it developed into the various romance languages spoken around the world today including Italian, French, Spanish, Portuguese, and Romanian. Many English words and abbreviations come from Latin too, such as: "vice versa," "a.m.," "p.m.," and "R.I.P." *Carpe diem*, the Latin phrase that means "live for the day," was first written by a famous Roman poet. And many of the specialized terms in science, law, and medicine come from Latin.

The Rise and Fall of the Roman Empire

Much of the world writes using an alphabet based on the uppercase letters written in Rome since 600 BCE, while the calendrical system has been only slightly modified from when Julius Caesar first devised it. Western law and government would be recognized by the ancients, too. Trials with a judge, jury, prosecutor, and defense attorney took place in Rome. The American system of government with laws voted on by the Senate and House of Representatives is modeled after the Roman Senate and the Assembly of Citizens. And anyone who has visited the U.S. Capitol in Washington, D.C., has seen examples of Roman-like architecture including the impressive columns and a central dome. Roman architects engineered a way of building arches, domes, columns, and vaults that was copied by other communities and cultures through time.

Yes, the Roman Empire did fall, but it also evolved. It evolved into the legacies we witness daily, and it lived on as the Eastern Roman Empire at Constantinople, which flourished as the Byzantine Empire until 1453 CE.

TIMELINE

c. 900–1000 BCE Settlements begin developing at site of Rome.
753 BCE According to legend, Rome is founded by Romulus and Remus.
509 BCE The Roman Republic is founded.
450 BCE The Laws of the Twelve Tables are issued.
343 BCE Rome begins its wars against the Samnites.
312 BCE Building of the first major Roman road, Via Appia, is started.
264 BCE The First Punic War between Rome and Carthage begins.
218 BCE The Second Punic War begins. Hannibal invades Italy.
149 BCE The Third Punic War begins. Carthage is destroyed by the end of the war.
Early 1st century BCE Rome controls the Mediterranean.
60 BCE Caesar, Crassus, and Pompey form the First Triumvirate.
46 BCE Julius Caesar becomes dictator.
44 BCE Julius Caesar is assassinated on March 15.
27 BCE Octavian is given title of Augustus and begins to rule the Roman Empire.
14 CE Augustus dies. Tiberius is named the next emperor.
37 CE Tiberius dies. Caligula becomes emperor.
41 CE Caligula is murdered. Caligula's uncle Claudius assumes power.
54 CE Claudius dies. Nero becomes emperor.
64 CE The Great Fire of Rome destroys two-thirds of the city. Nero blames and executes Christians.
79 CE Mount Vesuvius erupts.
96 CE The rule of Five Good Emperors begins with Nerva.
98 CE Nerva dies. Trajan becomes emperor.
114–16 CE The Roman Empire is at its greatest geographical area.
117 CE Trajan dies. Hadrian is named emperor.
120s CE Hadrian's Wall is constructed across northern England.
212 CE Peoples from throughout the Roman Empire are now considered citizens.
238–84 CE The Crisis of the Third Century marks a time of political and economic turmoil for the empire.

THE RISE AND FALL OF THE ROMAN EMPIRE

249 and 257 CE Terrible persecutions of Christians begin in these years.
284 CE Emperor Diocletian begins his reign.
293 CE The tetrarchy is complete. The empire is split with two rulers for each section.
303 CE The last widespread persecutions of Christians come to an end.
312 CE Constantine battles Maxentius and wins Rome.
313 CE Constantine and Licinius issue the Edict of Milan, which makes Christianity legal.
323–24 CE Constantine defeats Licinius, reunites the empire, and becomes sole ruler.
324 CE Constantine chooses Byzantium as his capital and renames it Constantinople.
395 CE Theodosius dies. The empire is completely divided into east and west.
410 CE Visigothic prince Alaric sacks Rome.
441–51 CE Huns invade Rome.
455 CE Rome is sacked for the second time by Vandal king Gaiseric.
476 CE The last Roman emperor is deposed by German general Odoacer.
1473 CE The Eastern Roman Empire, which lived on as the Byzantine Empire, comes to an end.

GLOSSARY

barbarian A person considered to be an outsider or not a citizen of Rome.
Colosseum Main amphitheater in Rome used by the public for various forms of entertainment.
consul One of two magistrates elected to serve yearly during the republic.
Curia Hostilia A meeting place where the Roman Senate conducted business.
dictator In ancient Rome, a magistrate who was given absolute power by the Senate in times of crisis.
forum A place in Roman towns where political and judicial business occurred.
ludi Public entertainment such as chariot races and gladiator shows.
magistrate A government official in charge of laws and other affairs of a locality.
military tribune An important military officer of the Roman Empire.
patrician A member by birth of a wealthy and elite family.
Pax Romana The period of peace and prosperity starting with the reign of Augustus and ending after the reign of Marcus Aurelius.
plebeian A common person during Roman times.
populus Romanus Adult male Roman citizens.
princeps A title, meaning first citizen, associated with emperors of Rome.
rex A male ruler, specifically a king.
Senate Group of elite men who advised first the kings of Rome and later, the emperors.
tetrarchy Joint rule by four people.
tribune A man elected by plebeian assemblies to represent the common people.
triumvirate Joint rule by three people.
via The Latin word for road.

FOR MORE INFORMATION

American Institute for Roman Culture
U.S. Academic Relations Office
3800 North Lamar Boulevard, Suite 730-174
Austin, TX 78756
(512) 772-1844
Website: http://www.romanculture.org
The American Institute for Roman Culture uses various educational tools and programs to promote public interest in the civilization of Rome.

Archaeological Institute of America
Boston University
656 Beacon Street
Boston, MA 02215
(617) 353-9361
Website: http://www.archaeological.org
The Archaeological Institute of America is dedicated to teaching the public about the history and cultures of the world through archaeological discovery.

The Classical Association of Canada (CAC)
    Department of Greek and Roman Studies
University of Victoria
Victoria, BC V8W 3P4
Canada
(250) 721-8528
Website: http://cac-scec.ca/wordpress
The CAC supports the study of ancient Greek and Roman civilizations and their significance in the modern world. It also promotes the teaching of classical languages in Canadian classrooms.

The Metropolitan Museum of Art
1000 Fifth Avenue (at 82nd Street)
New York, NY 10028
(212) 535-7710

For More Information

Website: http://www.metmuseum.org
The Met's vast collection includes more than seventeen thousand works of ancient Greek and Roman art, allowing visitors to gain a broad understanding of classical art and history.

Montreal Museum of Fine Arts
P.O. Box 3000, Station "H"
Montreal, QC H3G 2T9
Canada
(514) 285-2000
Website: http://www.mbam.qc.ca/en
The collection and exhibits at the Montreal Museum of Fine Arts include art from around the world and throughout history. Sculpture, jewelry, art, and other artifacts from ancient Rome are on display for public viewing.

New York University Center for Ancient Studies
100 Washington Square East, Room 503-o
New York, NY 10003
(212) 992-7978
Website: http://ancientstudies.as.nyu.edu/page/home
NYU's Center for Ancient Studies promotes interdisciplinary and cross-cultural study of the past.

WEBSITES

Because of the changing nature of Internet links, Rosen Publishing has developed an online list of websites related to the subject of this book. This site is updated regularly. Please use this link to access this list:
http://www.rosenlinks.com/RFE/rome

FOR FURTHER READING

Benoit, Peter. *Ancient Rome*. New York, NY: Children's Press, 2013.

Chrisp, Peter. *Explore 360 Pompeii*. Hauppauge, NY: Barron's Educational Series, Inc., 2015.

Cohn, Jessica. *The Ancient Romans*. New York, NY: Gareth Stevens Publishing, 2013.

Corrick, James. *The Bloody, Rotten Roman Empire: The Disgusting Details About Life in Ancient Rome*. North Mankato, MN: Capstone Press, 2011.

Deckker, Zilah. *Ancient Rome*. Washington, DC: National Geographic, 2007.

Dubois, Muriel L. *Ancient Rome: A Mighty Empire*. Mankato, MN: Capstone Press, 2012.

Hamen, Susan E. *Ancient Rome*. Mankato, MN: Essential Library, 2015.

Hawes, Alison. *A Roman Soldier's Handbook*. St. Catherine's, ON. 2011.

Hawes, Alison. *What the Romans Did for the World*. New York, NY: Crabtree Publishing, 2011.

James, Simon. *DK Eyewitness Books: Ancient Rome*. New York, NY: DK Children's Books, 2015.

Markel, Rita. *The Fall of the Roman Empire*. Minneapolis, MN: Lerner Publishing Group, 2008.

Nardo, Don. *The Roman Empire*. Farmington Hills, MI: Lucent Books, 2006.

Pistone, Nicholas, Giovanni Di Pasquale, and Matilde Bardi. *Art and Culture of Ancient Rome*. New York, NY: Rosen Publishing, 2010.

Samuels, Charlie. *Timeline of the Classical World*. New York, NY: Gareth Stevens Publishing, 2010.

Schomp, Virginia. *The Ancient Romans*. New York, NY: Marshall Cavendish Benchmark, 2009.

Scurman, Ike, and John Malam. *Ancient Roman Civilization*. New York, NY: Rosen Publishing, 2010.

BIBLIOGRAPHY

Andrews, Evan. "8 Ways Roads Helped Rome Rule the Ancient World." History, April 10, 2014 (http://www.history.com/news/history-lists/8-ways-roads-helped-rome-rule-the-ancient-world).

Baker, Simon. *Ancient Rome*. London, England: BBC Books, 2007.

Berndl, Klaus. *National Geographic Visual History of the World*. Washington, DC: National Geographic, 2005.

Boatwright, Mary T., Daniel J. Gargola, and Richard J. Talbert. *The Romans From Village to Empire*. New York, NY: Oxford University Press, 2004.

Bourbon, Fabio, and Anna M. Liberati. *Ancient Rome*. New York, NY: Barnes & Noble, 2004.

Discovery Channel School. *The Legacy of the Roman Empire*. Silver Spring, MD: Discovery Communications, Inc., 2004. DVD.

Freeman, Charles, J.F. Drinkwater, and Andrew Drummond. *The World of the Romans*. New York, NY: Oxford University Press, 1993.

Goodman, Martin. *The Roman World*. New York, NY: Routledge, 2012.

Grant, Michael. *The Founders of the Western World*. New York: Charles Scribner's Sons, 1991.

Grant, Michael. *From Rome to Byzantium*. New York, NY: Routledge, 1998.

Hadas, Moses. *Gibbon's The Decline and Fall of the Roman Empire: A Modern Abridgment*. New York, NY: G. P. Putnam's Sons, 1962.

Nardo, Don. *The End of Ancient Rome*. San Diego, CA: Greenhaven Press, Inc., 2001.

PBS. "The Roman Empire in the First Century" (http://www.pbs.org/empires/romans).

Poor, Bray. *When Rome Ruled*. Disc 3. National Geographic. Washington, DC: Vivendi Entertainment, 2011. DVD.

Reid, T R. "The Power and the Glory of the Roman Empire." *National Geographic*, July 1997 (http://archive.nationalgeographic.com/default.aspx?iid=54029#folio=2).

Reid, T R. "The World According to Rome." *National Geographic*, August 1997 (http://archive.nationalgeographic.com/?iid=54028#folio=54).

The Rise and Fall of the Roman Empire

Weber, Eugen Joseph. *The Western Tradition: Part 1*. South Burlington, VT: Annenberg/CPB, 2003. DVD.

Wayman, Erin. "The Secrets of Ancient Rome's Buildings." *Smithsonian*, November 16, 2011 (http://www.smithsonianmag.com/history/the-secrets-of-ancient-romes-buildings-234992).

Woolf, Greg, ed. *Cambridge Illustrated History of the Roman World*. Cambridge, England: Cambridge University Press, 2003.

Zwingle, Erla. "Italy Before the Romans." *National Geographic*, January 2005. (http://archive.nationalgeographic.com/default.aspx?iid=52135#folio=52).

INDEX

A
Aeneas, 8
Aeneid, 8
agriculture, 5, 6–7, 16, 19, 24, 34, 40
Alaric, 50
Alps, the, 6, 21
Antony, Mark, 29
Appian Way, 22

B
barbarians, 39–40, 48, 50
Britain, 4, 33, 38, 43
building and construction, 10, 11, 12, 22, 23–24, 25, 30, 32, 33, 34, 37, 38, 40, 52
Byzantium, 46–47, 52

C
Caesar, Julius, 27, 28–29, 52
Caligula, 32–33
Carthage, 20–23
Christianity, 35, 43, 45–47, 51
Claudius, 32–33
Cleopatra, 29
Colosseum, 10, 34
Constantine, 44–47
Constantinople, 47, 52
consuls, 15, 26, 27
Crassus, Marcus, 27
culture/art, 11–12, 13, 23, 25, 30–31, 33, 36
Curia Hostilia, 12

D
Diocletian, 41–44
disease, 38, 39, 40, 46

E
Edict of Milan, 45
Egypt, 4, 29, 43
Etruscans, 6, 20

F
Faliscans, 6
foederati, 48–49
Forum Romanum, 12

G
Gaiseric the Vandal, 51
Gauls, 20

H
Hadrian, 38, 40
Hannibal, 21–23
Horace, 30–31
Hostilius, Tullus, 10

I
Iron Age, 7
Italy, history of early people in, 6–7

J
Jews, 33, 35

Judaea, 33, 35

L

Latin language, 51
Latins, 6, 7
Laws of the Twelve Tables, 16
Lepidus, Marcus, 29
Licinius, 45

M

magistrates, 15, 18, 29
Marcus, Ancus, 10
Marcus Aurelius, 38
Maxentius, 44
Maximian, 42
Mediterranean Sea, 6, 23, 27
military, 18–23, 26, 29, 30, 33, 34, 35, 36, 37–38, 39, 40, 42, 45, 48

N

Nero, 33, 34, 36
Nerva, Marcus Cocceius, 36–37

O

Octavian/Augustus, 28–30, 32, 33
Odoacer, Flavius, 51
opus caementicium, 10
Ovid, 30–31

P

Pantheon, 10, 38
paterfamilias, 17
patricians, 13–14, 15, 16, 19, 36
Pax Romana, 31, 36, 39
Pius, Antoninus, 38
plebians, 16, 26
Pliny, 31
Pompey, Gaius, 27
Pompilius, Numa, 10
populous Romanus, 13, 15
Praetorian Guard, 32–33
Punic Wars, 20–23

R

religion, 10, 11–12, 15, 18, 23–25, 35, 36, 43, 45–47, 51
Remus, 8–9, 12
Roman Empire
    attacks against, 39–40, 42, 48, 49, 50–51
    decline and fall of, 39–52
    emperors, 29–31, 32–38
    influence of, 5, 51–52
    from republic to empire, 29–30
    size/growth of, 4–5, 19–20, 25, 26, 34–36, 37–38, 40
    split into Eastern and Western, 46–48
Roman Republic, 15–25, 26–27, 29
Rome, early history of, 7–12, 13–14
Romulus, 8–10, 12
Romulus Augustulus, 51

INDEX

S

Sabines, 6
Samnites, 6, 19–20, 22
Senate, 10, 12, 14, 16, 23, 26, 27, 29, 30, 32, 33, 36, 37, 47, 52
Sicily, 20
slaves, 16, 40

T

Tarquinius Priscus, Lucius, 10
Tarquin the Proud (Lucius Tarquinius Suberbus), 10, 15
tetrarchy, 42, 44
Theodosius, 47
Tiberius, 32
Tiber River, 7, 9, 10
Trajan, 37–38
Trojan War, 8
Tullius, Servius, 10

U

Umbrians, 6, 12, 20

V

Virgil, 8, 30
Visigoths, 50

The Rise and Fall of the Roman Empire

ABOUT THE AUTHOR

Lisa Idzikowski is a writer from Milwaukee, Wisconsin. She loves science, history, and living near Lake Michigan. When she isn't reading, researching or writing, Lisa works on her native plant garden to attract birds, bees, and butterflies.

PHOTO CREDITS

Cover, p. 1 Stefano Pellicciari/Shiutterstock.com; p. 4 Apic/Hulton Archive/Getty Images; p. 7 DEA/Pubbli Aer Foto/De Agostini/Getty Images; pp. 8, 42 Mondadori Portfolio/Hulton Fine Art Collection/Getty Images; p. 11 Digitaler Lumpensammier/Moment/Getty Images; p. 12, 46 DEA Picture Library/De Agostini/Getty Images; p. 14 Culture Club/Hulton Archive/Getty Images; pp. 17, 30 Print Collector/Hulton Arcive/Getty Images; p. 18 De Agostini Picture Library/Getty Images; pp. 21, 31 DEA/G. Dagli Orti/De Agostini/Getty Images; p. 24 De Agostini/V. Pirozzi/De Agostini/Getty Images; p. 28 Leemage/Hulton Fine Art Collection/Getty Images; p. 34 Maxime Bermond/Moment/Getty Images; p. 37 Independent Picture Service/Universal Images Group/Getty Images; p. 41 De Agostini/W. Buss/Getty Images; p. 44, 49 PHAS/Universal Images Group/Getty Images; interior pages background image © iStockphoto.com/somnuk

Designer: Brian Garvey; Editor: Shalini Saxena; Photo Researcher: Nicole Baker